My First French Picture Dictionary

Illustrated by Nick Sharratt

Written by Christine Mabileau and Irene Yates

Consultant Editors Natasha Farrant and Ginny Lapage

Collins

An imprint of HarperCollinsPublishers

Managing Editor: Jilly MacLeod
Art Director: Rachel Hamdi
Design Consultant: Sophie Stericker
Cover Designers: Susi Martin, Sonia Dobie
Designers: Holly Mann, Sarah Borny

First published in 2001 by HarperCollins*Children's Books*,
a division of HarperCollins*Publishers* Ltd
77-85 Fulham Palace Road, London W6 8JB

The HarperCollins website address is:
www.**fire**and**water**.com

On-line Support for Schools and Colleges
www.**Collins**Education.com

ISBN 0 00 198405 5

2 4 6 8 10 9 7 5 3 1

Printed in Hong Kong

Contents

How to use this book

Children love playing with words, and learning a new language can be lots of fun. This colourful dictionary is specially designed to help you introduce your child to French. With your help, your child will learn key words from a range of familiar situations, discovering new sounds along the way. They will also start to recognize some of the differences and similarities between French and English.

First steps to learning French

As soon as they are comfortable expressing themselves in their own language, children are ready to learn a new one. To get the best out of this book, sit with your child and encourage them to look at the pictures, to say the French words as often as possible,

Tom

Elisha

Jake

Read the heading out loud so your child knows the context of the French words.

Point to the picture, then run your finger along the French words, from left to right, saying the words out loud. Ask you child to repeat the words, not forgetting to say the short word in front.

Compare the French word with the English, pointing out the similarities as well as the differences between the two languages.

Look for me on every page – sometimes you will have to look very hard! It's fun to see what I'm doing.

Having fun at playschool

l'ordinateur
computer

la maîtresse
teacher

le livre
book

les ciseaux
scissors

la peinture
paint

le pinceau
paintbrush

la colle
glue

les crayons
crayons

12

and to answer all the questions. Come back to the book time and time again, so your child absorbs the new sounds and learns to associate the French words with the pictures.

Questions and answers

Nick Sharrat's lively scenes will help your child to memorize the French words by putting them into context. They also offer plenty of scope for further questions, so you can encourage your child to practice speaking their newly learned words. For your own guidance, there is a pronunciation guide at the back of the book.

Ask the questions, encouraging your child always to answer in French. (The answers will be words featured on the spread.)

Encourage your child to point out and name real objects around them whenever possible.

Make up your own questions, based on what's going on in the picture. Once your child has learned about colours and numbers (see pages 40-43), you can incorporate these in your questions too, for example, "How many paintbrushes can you count?"

Learning the names of the characters will add to the fun your child gets from using this book.

Ask your child to match objects in the main picture with those shown on the left, and vice versa. When looking for an object, encourage your child always to use its French name.

Lucy

Taz

Amy

5

Fun and games at home

la porte
door

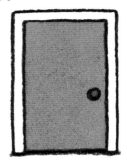

la fenêtre
window

la chaise
chair

le canapé
sofa

le coussin
cushion

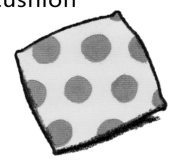

la pendule
clock

la télévision
television

le téléphone
telephone

6

Look at me!

la tête
head

les cheveux
hair

le visage
face

le nez
nose

les yeux
eyes

les oreilles
ears

les dents
teeth

la bouche
mouth

le cou
neck

l'épaule
shoulder

What do you smell things with?

8

Come to my birthday party

le ballon
balloon

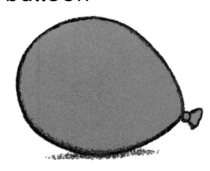

le masque
mask

le cadeau
present

le chapeau en papier
party hat

la glace
ice cream

le gâteau
cake

le jus de fruit
fruit juice

les bonbons
sweets

Having fun at playschool

l'ordinateur
computer

le livre
book

la peinture
paint

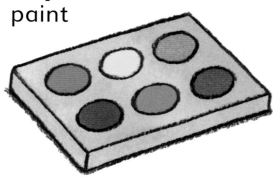

les crayons
crayons

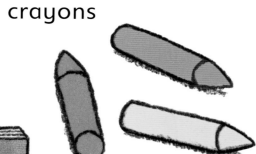

la maîtresse
teacher

les ciseaux
scissors

le pinceau
paintbrush

la colle
glue

What do we like to wear?

la chemise
shirt

la veste
jacket

la robe
dress

le pantalon
trousers

la jupe
skirt

le short
shorts

les chaussettes
socks

les chaussures
shoes

What do
you like to wear
best?

14

What do you wear on your hands?

le pyjama
pyjamas

la chemise de nuit
nightie

le caleçon
pants

la culotte
knickers

le pull
jumper

le T-shirt
T-shirt

le bonnet
hat

les gants
gloves

Let's play in the garden

la tondeuse
lawnmower

la brouette
wheelbarrow

le papillon
butterfly

l'oiseau
bird

l'arrosoir
watering can

le vélo
bike

la pataugeoire
paddling pool

la fleur
flower

Take a walk down our street

la maison
house

le magasin
shop

l'agent de police
policeman

la route
road

la voiture
car

le lampadaire
street light

le fauteuil roulant
wheelchair

les feux
traffic light

Where do you go to buy things?

Things that go

les rollers
rollerblades

le camion
lorry

la moto
motorbike

le bus
bus

l'excavateur
digger

le camion benne
dumper truck

le bateau
boat

le skateboard
skateboard

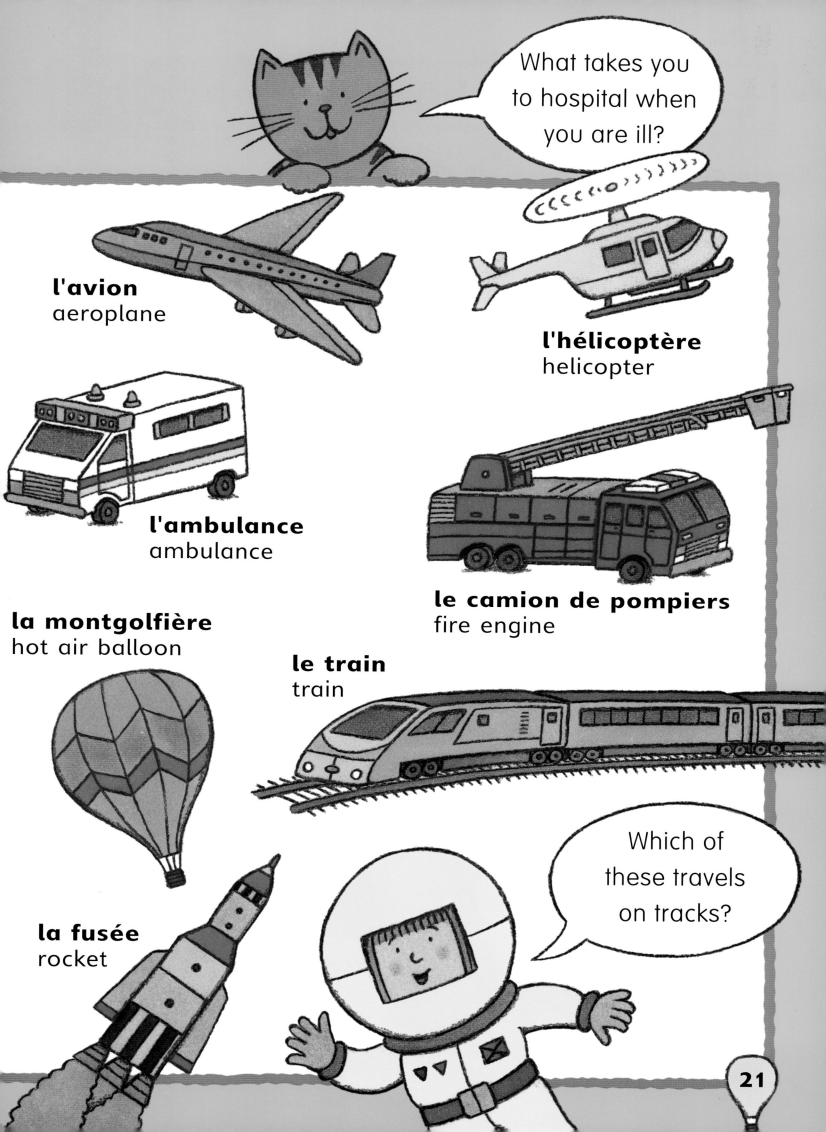

Let's go to the toy shop

le puzzle
jigsaw puzzle

le camion
truck

le garage
garage

la maison de poupées
doll's house

l'ours en peluche
teddy bear

la poupée
doll

la marionnette
puppet

les cubes
blocks

At the supermarket

le bocal
jar

le sac
bag

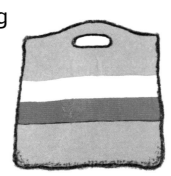

la boîte de conserve
tin

le panier
basket

le caddy
trolley

l'argent
money

la caisse
checkout

la bouteille
bottle

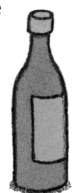

24

Food to help me grow

les fruits
fruit

les légumes
vegetables

le riz
rice

le hamburger
hamburger

les frites
chips

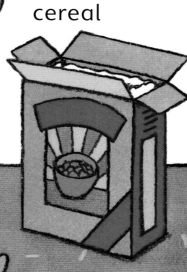

les spaghetti
spaghetti

les céréales
cereal

What do you
eat for breakfast?

26

Take me to the pet shop

le lapin
rabbit

le hamster
hamster

le chaton
kitten

le chiot
puppy

le poisson rouge
goldfish

le panier
basket

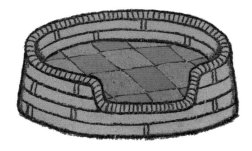

la cage
cage

la perruche
budgie

What's in the park?

le toboggan
slide

la balançoire
swing

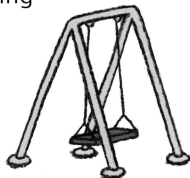

la poussette
buggy

la cage à grimper
climbing frame

le banc
bench

l'arbre
tree

le chien
dog

le canard
duck

Big beasts and minibeasts

le kangourou
kangaroo

le lion
lion

la girafe
giraffe

le panda
panda

l'éléphant
elephant

le crocodile
crocodile

la baleine
whale

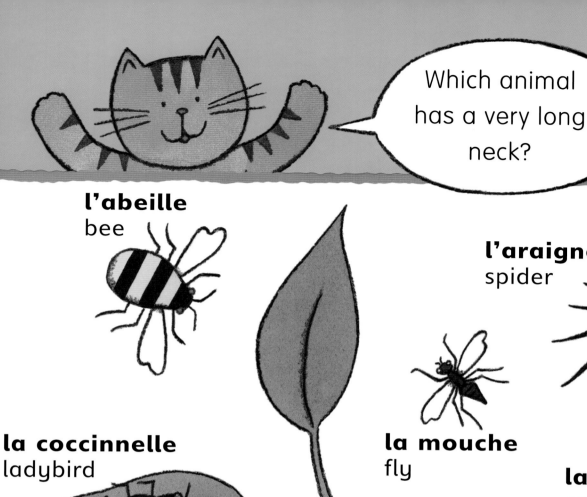

Which animal has a very long neck?

l'abeille
bee

l'araignée
spider

la coccinnelle
ladybird

la mouche
fly

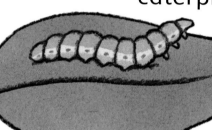

la chenille
caterpillar

l'escargot
snail

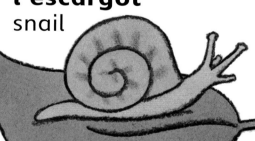

le scarabée
beetle

What carries its home on its back?

le ver de terre
worm

Down on the farm

Le fermier
farmer

le tracteur
tractor

la poule
hen

l'agneau
lamb

le cheval
horse

la vache
cow

la barrière
gate

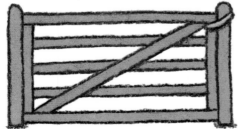

le foin
hay

34

A sunny day at the seaside

le coquillage
shell

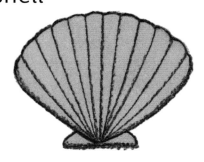

le crabe
crab

la mouette
seagull

le château de sable
sand castle

le ballon de plage
beach ball

la vague
wave

le seau
bucket

la pelle
spade

See what we can do!

il saute
he jumps

il marche
he walks

elle court
she runs

elle applaudit
she claps

elle porte
she carries

What is the girl with the box doing?

il peint
he paints

ils dansent they dance

38

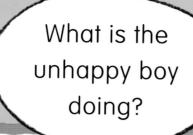
What is the unhappy boy doing?

il chante
he sings

il rit
he laughs

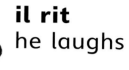

elle brosse
she brushes

elle coupe
she cuts

il pleure
he cries

elle mange
she eats

elle boit
she drinks

Colours are everywhere

violet
purple

rouge
red

noir
black

bleu
blue

jaune
yellow

What colour is the bouncy castle?

Come and count with me

1 un

2 deux

3 trois

How many windows does this house have?

4 quatre

5 cinq

Count the spots on the ladybird.

6 six

7 sept

8 huit

9 neuf

10 dix

lundi
Monday

mardi
Tuesday

mercredi
Wednesday

jeudi
Thursday

vendredi
Friday

samedi
Saturday

dimanche
Sunday

le jour
day

la nuit
night

What day
of the week
is it?

What makes you put up your umbrella?

le soleil
sun

la pluie
rain

le vent
wind

la neige
snow

How the words sound

A

aeroplane	l'avion – lavy**on**
ambulance	l'ambulance – l**an**bul**an**s
arm	le bras – **le** bra

B

bag	le sac – **le** sak
balloon	le ballon – **le** bal**on**
basket	le panier – **le** panyay
beach ball	le ballon de plage – **le** bal**on** de pla**j**
bee	l'abeille – labay
beetle	le scarabée – **le** scarabay
bench	le banc – **le** ba**n**
bike	le vélo – **le** vaylo
bird	l' oiseau – lwazo
biscuits	les biscuits – lay beeskwee
black	noir – nwar
blocks	les cubes – lay k**ub**
blue	bleu – bl**e**
boat	le bateau – **le** bato
book	le livre – **le** leevr
bottle	la bouteille – la bootay
bottom	le derrière – **le** deryayr
bread	le pain – **le** p**in**
brown	marron – mar**on**
brushes, she	elle brosse – el bros

bucket	le seau – **le** so
budgie	la perruche – la per**u**sh
buggy	la poussette – la poosset
bus	le bus – **le** b**u**s
butterfly	le papillon – **le** papeey**on**

C

cage	la cage – la ka**j**
cake	le gâteau – **le** gato
car	la voiture – la vwat**u**r
carries, she	elle porte – el port
caterpillar	la chenille – la sheneey
cereal	les céréales – lay sayrayhal
chair	la chaise – la shez
checkout	la caisse – la kess
cheese	le fromage – **le** froma**j**
chicken	le poulet – **le** poolay
chips	les frites – lay freet
claps, she	elle applaudit – el aplodee
climbing frame	la cage à grimper – la ka**j** a gr**in**pay
clock	la pendule – la p**an**d**u**l
computer	l'ordinateur – l'ordinater
cow	la vache – la vash
crab	le crabe – **le** krab
cries, he	il pleure – eel pler
crocodile	le crocodile – **le** krokodeel
cushion	le coussin – **le** koss**in**
cuts, she	elle coupe – el koop

D

dance, they	ils dansent – eel d**an**s
day	le jour – **le** joor
digger	l'excavateur – lexkavat**e**r
dog	le chien – **le** shee**in**
doll	la poupée – la poopay
dolls house	la maison de poupées – la mayzon de poopay
door	la porte – la port
dress	la robe – la rob
drinks, she	elle boit – el bwa
duck	le canard – **le** kanar
dumper truck	le camion benne – **le** kamy**on** ben

E

ears	les oreilles – *lay zoray*
eats, she	elle mange – *el manj*
eggs	les œufs – *lay ze*
eight	huit – *weet*
elbow	le coude – *le kood*
elephant	l'éléphant – *lelefan*
eyes	les yeux – *layzye*

F

face	le visage – *le veezaj*
farmer	le fermier – *le fayrmyay*
finger	le doigt – *le dwa*
fire engine	le camion de pompiers – *le kamyon de ponpyay*
fish	le poisson – *le pwasson*
five	cinq – *sink*
flower	la fleur – *la fler*
fly	la mouche – *la moosh*
foot	le pied – *le pyay*
four	quatre – *katr*
Friday	vendredi – *vandredee*
fruit	les fruits – *lay frwee*
fruit juice	le jus de fruit – *le ju de frwee*

G

garage	le garage – *le garaj*
gate	la barrière – *la baryayr*
giraffe	la girafe – *la jeeraf*
gloves	les gants – *lay gan*
glue	la colle – *la kol*
goldfish	le poisson rouge – *le pwasson rooj*
green	vert – *vayr*

H

hair	les cheveux – *lay sheve*
hamburger	le hamburger – *le hamburger*
hamster	le hamster – *le amster*
hand	la main – *la min*
hat	le bonnet – *le bonay*
hay	le foin – *le fwin*
head	la tête – *la tet*
helicopter	l'hélicoptère – *lelikoptayr*
hen	la poule – *la pool*
horse	le cheval – *le sheval*
hot air balloon	la montgolfière – *la mongolfyear*
house	la maison – *la mayzon*

I J

ice cream	la glace – *la glass*
jacket	la veste – *la vest*

jar	le bocal – *le bokal*
jigsaw puzzle	le puzzle – *le puzl*
jumps, he	il saute – *eel sot*
jumper	le pull – *le pul*

K

kangaroo	le kangourou – *le kangooroo*
kitten	le chaton – *le shaton*
knee	le genou – *le jenoo*
knickers	la culotte – *la kulot*

L

ladybird	la coccinnelle – *la cokseenel*
lamb	l'agneau – *lanyo*
laughs, he	il rit – *eel ree*
lawnmower	la tondeuse – *la tonderz*
leg	la jambe – *la janb*
lion	le lion – *le lyon*
lorry	le camion – *le kamyon*

M

mask	le masque – *le mask*
milk	le lait – *le lay*
Monday	lundi – *landee*
money	l'argent – *larjan*
motor bike	la moto – *la moto*
mouth	la bouche – *la bush*

N

night	la nuit – *la nwee*
night-dress	la chemise de nuit – *la shemeez de nwee*
nine	neuf – *nerf*
nose	le nez – *le nay*
neck	le cou – *le koo*

O

one	un – *an*
orange	orange – *oranj*

P

paddling pool	la pataugeoire – *la patojwar*
paints, he	il peint – *eel p**in***
paintbrush	le pinceau – *le p**in**so*
panda	le panda – *le p**an**da*
pants	le caleçon – *le kals**on***
party hat	le chapeau en papier – *le shapo **an** papyay*
pen	les crayons – *lay kray**on***
pink	rose – *rose*
pizza	la pizza – *la peedza*
policeman	l'agent de police – *la**jan** d**e** police*
present	le cadeau – *le kado*
puppet	la marionnette – *la maryonet*
puppy	le chiot – *le shyo*
purple	violet – *vyolay*
pyjamas	le pyjama – *le pee**j**ama*

R

rabbit	le lapin – *le lap**in***
rain	la pluie – *la plwee*
red	rouge – *roo**j***
rice	le riz – *le ree*
road	la route – *la root*
rocket	la fusée – *la f**u**zay*
rollerblades	les rollers – *lay roller*
runs, she	elle court – *el koor*

S

sandcastle	le château de sable – *le shato d**e** sable*
Saturday	samedi – *sa**m**edee*
scissors	les ciseaux – *lay seezo*
seagull	la mouette – *la mwet*
seven	Sept – *set*
shell	le coquillage – *le kokeeya**j***
shirt	la chemise – *la shemeez*
shoes	les chaussures – *lay shoss**ur***
shop	le magasin – *le magaz**in***
shorts	le short – *le short*
shoulder	l'épaule – *laypol*
sings, he	il chante – *eel sh**ant***
six	six – *seess*
skateboard	le skateboard – *le skateboard*
skirt	la jupe – *la **j**up*
slide	le toboggan – *le tobog**an***
snail	l'escargot – *leskargo*
snow	la neige – *la ne**j***
socks	les chaussettes – *lay shosset*
sofa	le canapé – *le kanapay*

(continued)

spade	la pelle – *la pel*
spaghetti	les spaghetti – *lay spaghetti*
spider	l'araignée – *laraynay*
street light	le lampadaire – *le lanpadayr*
sun	le soleil – *le soley*
Sunday	dimanche – *dee**man**sh*
sweets	les bonbons – *lay b**onbon***
swing	la balançoire – *la bal**an**swar*

T

teacher	la maîtresse – *la maytrayss*
teddy bear	l'ours en peluche – *loors an pel**ush***
teeth	les dents – *lay d**an***
telephone	le téléphone – *le telefon*
television	la télévision – *la televeezy**on***
ten	dix – *deess*
three	trois – *trwa*
thumb	le pouce – *le pooss*
Thursday	jeudi – ***je**dee*
tin	la boîte de conserve – *la bwat d**e k**onserv*
toe	l'orteil – *lortay*
tractor	le tracteur – *le trakter*
traffic light	les feux – *lay f**e***
train	le train – *le tr**in***
tree	l'arbre – *larbr*
trolley	le caddy – *le kadee*
trousers	le pantalon – *le p**an**tal**on***
truck	le camion – *le kamyon*
T-shirt	le T-shirt – *le tee-shirt*
Tuesday	mardi – *mardee*
tummy	le ventre – *le v**an**tr*
two	deux – *de*

U V W

vegetables	les légumes – *lay layg**um***
walks, he	il marche – *eel marsh*
watering can	l'arrosoir – *larozwar*
wave	la vague – *la vague*
Wednesday	mercredi – *mayrcredee*
whale	la baleine – *la balen*
wheelbarrow	la brouette – *la broohet*
wheelchair	le fauteuil roulant – *le fot**ey** rool**an***
white	blanc – *blan*
wind	le vent – *le v**an***
window	la fenêtre – *la f**e**netr*
worm	le ver de terre – *le vayr d**e** tayr*

X Y Z

yellow	jaune – *jon*
yoghurt	le yaourt – *le yahoort*